How Cat and Dog

Written and illustrated by Shoo Rayner

Contents

Collins

How to draw Cat

Start with a big,
round shape for
the head.

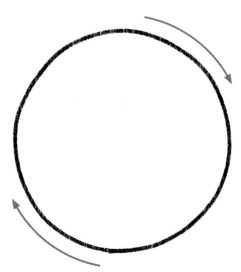

Draw a line up and down on the left side.

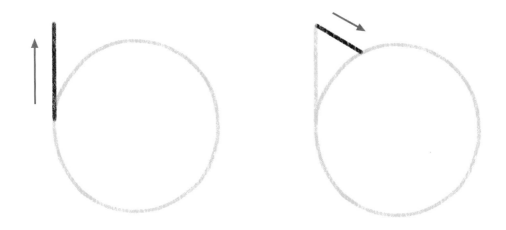

Repeat on the right side.

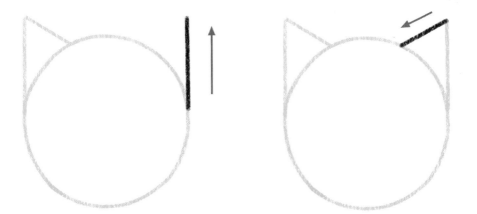

Draw a ring below each ear.

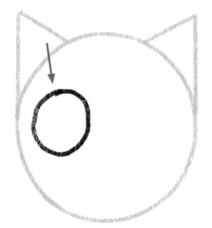 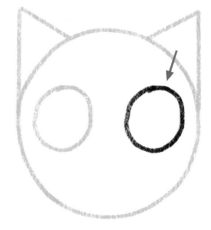

Put dots in the rings.

Draw an oval between the rings and a line down from it.

Add the smile like a segment of lemon and three lines on each cheek.

Draw a box beside the head.

Then add four legs.

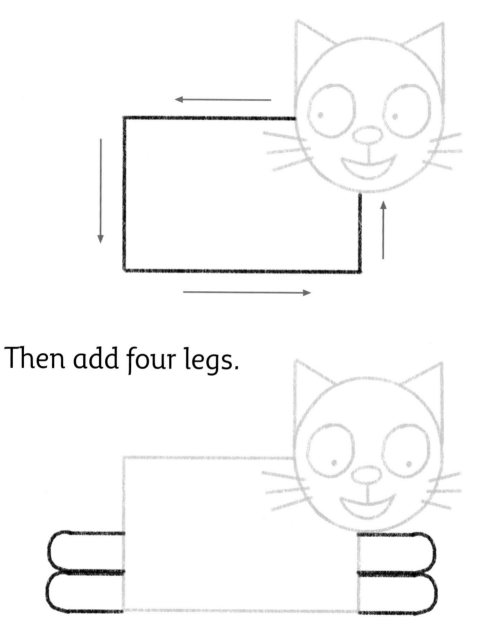

Draw short lines to make four paws.

Don't forget the long tail!

How to draw Dog

Start with a raindrop shape.

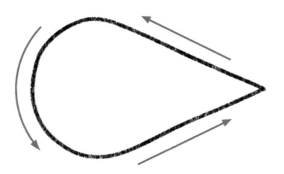

For the left ear, draw a curved line up
and back on the left side.

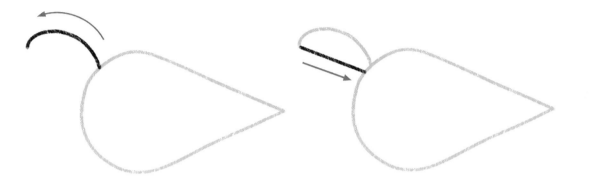

Repeat for the right ear.

Draw a ring below each ear.

Put dots inside the rings!

Draw a ring to
make a nose.

Then draw a smile.

Draw a box attached to the head.

Then add four legs.

Draw short lines to make four paws.

Don't forget the pointed tail!

Dog spies Cat.   Cat spies Dog.

Dog chases Cat down the street.

Woof!

Zoom! Cat escapes from Dog.

But where can Cat hide?

How to draw a tree

Draw a cloud shape.

Fill the cloud shape with leaves.

Draw branches on your tree.

Finish the sides of
the branches and
draw the trunk to
the ground.

Draw zigzag lines
to make the roots.

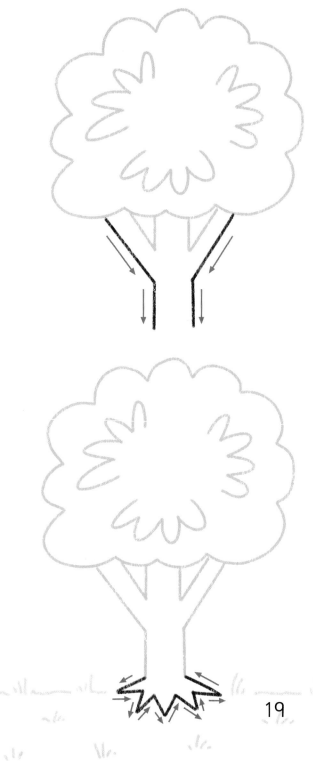

Now Cat can disappear in the tall tree!

Dog can see Cat, but he can't reach her.

Now you can make and colour your own Cat and Dog book!

Drawing Cat and Dog

Cat

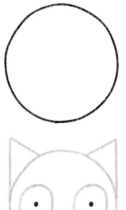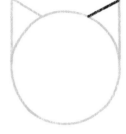

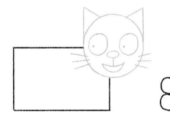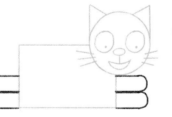

Tree

Dog

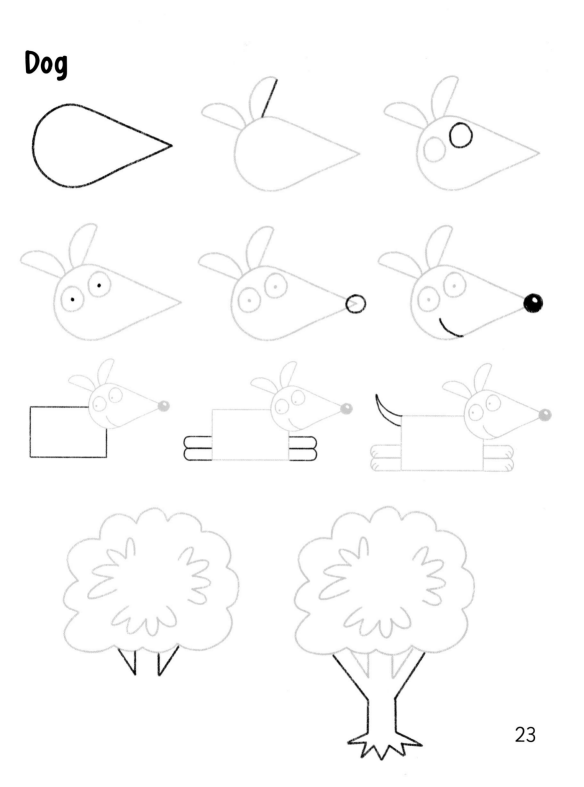

After reading

Letters and Sounds: Phase 5

Word count: 254

Focus phonemes: /ar/ a, /or/ aw, our, al, /ow/ ou, /ai/ a-e, /e/ ea, /igh/ i-e, i , / ee/ ea, /ure/ our, /oa/ o, ow, o-e

Common exception word: where, of, to, the, put

Curriculum links: Art and design: to develop a wide range of art and design techniques in using colour, pattern, texture, line, shape, form and space

National Curriculum learning objectives: Spoken language: listen and respond appropriately to adults and their peers; Reading/Word reading: respond speedily with the correct sound to graphemes (letters or groups of letters) including, where applicable, alternative sounds for graphemes, read other words of more than one syllable that contain taught GPCs, read aloud accurately books that are consistent with their developing phonic knowledge; Reading/Comprehension: understand ... the books they can already read ... by drawing on what they already know or on background information and vocabulary provided by the teacher

Developing fluency

- Your child may enjoy hearing you read the book. Model reading instructions.
- Now ask your child to read some of the book again, reading the instructions with appropriate expression.

Phonic practice

- Ask your child to sound out each of the following words:

  d/r/aw   f/our   t/al/l
- Ask your child:
  - Can you tell me which sound is the same in each word? (/or/)
  - Can you remember different ways to write the phoneme /or/? Can you point to the grapheme (letter or letters) that make the /or/ sound in each word? (aw, our, al)
  - Can you think of any other words with the /or/ sound in them? (e.g. *claw, pour, fall*)

Extending vocabulary

- Look at page 10. Ask your child if they can think of another word that could be used instead of **ring**? (e.g. *circle*)